OPEN SKY CREATIONS

Unleashing Your Inner Artist with Acrylic Landscapes

Elaine Ellis

Table of Contents

CHAPTER ONE

INTRODUCTION

Scene painting suggests the depiction of common view, like dusk, seas, mountains, valleys, woodlands, fields, water bodies, dales, and beach front locale in workmanship. Such designs can be painted whenever of the day, each time keeping an eye on the enchanting significance of that hour! While most plans get the exemplification of still parts, now and again they could merge living things like creatures, birds, or even people. Scene painting is an old workmanship that started during the fourth hundred years in China. Also, scene painting thoughts have a significant significance during renaissance time when specialists depicted the European "Restoration" and defended it for the approaching ages.

HEAD STANDARDS FOR SCENE PAINTING

Painting like is a long association that requires huge length of planning in any case, one can accomplish impeccability by seeing these four basic guidelines.

• Central center interests: For the most part called the focal centers, central focuses are the bits of a creation that quickly get one's eye. Adolescents can attract an association to plot these central bright lights on the material. Besides, experts can draw an optional spot of get together for ideal impact.

• S-shapes: To move the eye around the creation, specialists utilize a S-shape or talk Z-shape connecting parts from basic central focuses to optional central spots.

• Skyline: The situation of a skyline holds central significance as it ties the chance of a material together. For instance, on the off chance that the specialists draw a Sea view, they should keep the skyline close to the most critical spot of the material. Then again, it ought to be kept low while drawing the sky.

• Clear: Areas of strength for changes and remarkable division raise the general feel of the material. This is the explanation that all settled specialists use groupings of blues and orange components to make a 3D picture in a scene painting.

SCENE PAINTING TIPS

While there are no deeply grounded conditions for scene painting, there are four focal rules for achieving an astonishing design near the end. For instance,

• Perceive the fundamental pieces of a scene going before beginning your design. Envision your last look and make light draws in to stay away from any changes.

• Constantly select a piece that feels wide. Keep in mind, your synthesis is the portrayal of your imaginative brain.

• Avoid going through and exaggerating a scene painting. Pick fitting feelings and subtleties for the work.

• Achieve your course of action by making light to dull progress. Make importance on the material by utilizing features, mid-tones, and shadows.

• Utilize a charcoal pencil to draw on your under painting on material.

FOUR COLOSSAL BITS OF SCENE PAINTING

It is essential to see the value in the basics of scene painting to secure the best outcomes. There are enormous bits of scene painting that should b went before beginning the joint effort.

• Forward looking locale

• Center ground

• Foundation

• Skyline

CHAPTER TWO

HOW TO CHANGE A SCENE PAINTING

Exceptional synthesis is the foundation of a reasonable scene; in any case, it requires a few explicit information. The sky, land, main concerns, and different parts need strategy for exactness and further created results. The surface, beat, heading of lines, plans, partitions, viewpoints, and space division are fundamental for managing a scene's general quality plan and visual appeal. A magnificent rule for ideal piece is the "Rule of Thirds", i.e., the place of combination of the scene ought not to be in the middle. Considering everything, it ought to be open at the gathering of the thirds.

SUPPLIES EXPECTED TO PAINT ON MATERIAL

Scene painting materials required:

• Significant Acrylic paints in various tones or Winsor and Newton able quality chambers. For spending plan cheerful expert quality paint try Mont Marte Paint Set. Fundamental varieties you really need as an adolescent at acrylic painting of sprouts on material merge titanium white, quinacridone red, ultramarine blue, phthalo blue, titanium buff, cadmium orange, consumed splendid, cadmium red, phthalo green, sap green, unpleasant sienna, cadmium ceaselessly yellow ocre.

• Paint Brushes of different sizes and shapes

• Material or a gem surface such a wood sheets or watercolor book.

• Collection blending reach or expendable compasses.

• Compartment for water can be a cup, bowl, or a pointless yogurt holder or food putting away bowl.

• To clean brushes - hold your brushes a water and fluid dishwashing cleaning specialist plan and wash it with clean running water a short period of time later. Meticulously smooth the strands of the brush to kill any advancement with paper towels or delicate material.

• Discretionary: Easel for more open to painting.

• Range collection blending guide

• Range sharp edge

• Charcoal pencil

HOW TO BEGIN FANNING OUT A SCENE

There are three essential stages prior to starting a scene painting:

• Utilization of a colored foundation: This step is colossal for a bound together tone of the material. Besides, it gives a decent under attempt to satisfy scene.

• Draw the foundation: Drawing a foundation sketch is useful in reviewing what's going on of parts. 3B pencils are ideally suited for making these obnoxious depictions.

• Mark tones: Spread out the dull and the light region of an association. Utilize different dull and light tones to move toward region of a scene for commonplace look.

KINDS OF SCENE WORKS OF ART

There are three focal sorts of scene workmanship:

• Legitimate Scene Craftsmanship: Scene that seem, by all accounts, to be reality

• Impressionistic Scene Workmanship: Bring out feelings and conclusions

• Dynamic Scene Workmanship: Doesn't address reality rather go presumably as a pathway to the excursion of considering.

A talented specialist should pick a style prior to beginning to paint.

WHAT SORT OF PAINT BRUSH FOR PAINTING ON MATERIAL

While arranging scene, take a stab at utilizing the accompanying paint brushes:

• Round brushes: for small lines and specifying.

• Level brushes: best for over generalized terms and more extensive petals.

• Filbert brushes: are valuable for mixing and creating adjusted shapes.

• Liner brushes: are utilized for fine subtleties and sensitive lines.

• Fan brushes: are valuable for creating surfaces and foliage.

Note that regularly level brushes are utilized to paint with acrylic paints for best outcomes.

THE SPECIALTY OF SCENE PAINTING

Scene painting is a craftsmanship that requires abilities and inventiveness. Gone are the days when a couple of choices were free for acrylic scene works of art. While these decisions have added to the appeal of scenes and investigated further elements of compositions (like contemporary fine art), it has additionally brought up a few difficult issues for the painters. Which tone is reasonable? Which range is great for a particular landscape? What materials do I have to begin acrylic painting? What is the initial step of acrylic painting? Furthermore, in particular, what materials do I have to begin laying out a scene? This book will answer every one of your inquiries and furnish you with the most straightforward yet innovative acrylic scene painting thoughts for your next project! You will likewise partake in the absolute most fascinating bits of workmanship like Best Artistic creation Thoughts on Material for Novices and Simple things to paint on material. Before we begin let's find out about a few as often as possible posed inquiries for blossom painting thoughts.

COLORS UTILIZED FOR THIS COMPOSITION

For this painting I utilized Winsor and Newton Proficient Acrylic Paints.

1. Titanium white

2. Consumed sienna

3. Yellow ochre

4. Cadmium yellow

5. Cadmium red

6. Alizarin red

7. Ultramarine blue

8. Phthalo green

BRUSHES

As far as brushes, there are many shapes, sizes, and types to choose from. Each brush offers various impacts and is appropriate for various painting methods.

For expansive brush strokes and filling huge regions, level brushes are great. Round brushes, then again, are ideal for itemized work and lines.

Fan brushes are valuable for mixing and making intriguing textural impacts. As a novice, consider beginning with an essential arrangement of brushes in various sizes and shapes to investigate what turns out best for your style. Picking the right tones and brushes is pivotal to the painting system, establishing the vibe for your work and giving it its interesting person. Keep in mind, while the apparatuses are fundamental, your imagination and vision really reinvigorate your craft.

CHAPTER THREE

BIT BY BIT GUIDE LAYING OUT A SCENE IN ACRYLICS

Prepare to rejuvenate the lively magnificence of scenes on your material as I tell you the best way to lay out a scene in acrylics that includes a mountain and a stream.

ILLUSTRATING THE SYTHESIS

Before you begin painting, contemplating the critical components of your scene composition is fundamental. In this artwork, I have made an 'S' shape, with the waterway and mountain becoming the overwhelming focus. I moved the foundation mountain towards the middle left so the stream drives the eye towards it. The foundation mountain is the super point of convergence in the artistic creation. Feel free to move components around and change what you see you don't need to duplicate your reference makegraph unequivocally exactly as a matter of fact I would firmly prompt against it. I painted this work of art on an 8" x 10" material board prepared with an unmistakable gesso. I chose not to add layers of gesso as I preferred the pale, gritty tone of the cloth I was painting. I framed the synthesis with consumed sienna blended in with a touch of water.

HINDERING IN THE CANVAS

Whenever I have framed the structure, I next ponder the qualities in the scene I'm painting. Values allude to how light or dim a subject is, and the overall guideline is that we will track down our haziest darks and our lightest lights in the forefront. As expanses of land retreat into the distances, darks become fewer darks, and lights are not really light.

LAY OUT THE MOST OBSCURE DARKS AND LIGHTEST LIGHTS

By generally painting in the primary region of the shadows first in our acrylic scene painting procedures, it will make it a lot simpler to paint the regions in light a short time later. It likewise makes blending the tones for the light regions more easy and makes air profundity in your composition.

I paint the shadows behind the scenes mountain utilizing a blend of ultramarine blue, consumed sienna, titanium white and a touch of alizarin dark red. I remember that the shadows in the mountain are lighter in esteem than the shadows in the forefront. As I work my direction towards the forefront, those shadows are getting hazier thus I utilize less titanium white in my shadow blend. I likewise edge the paint blend on the blue side and I make broken variety by not completely combining the varieties as one to permit a portion of the singular shades to come through.

PAINTING THE SKY AND MISTS

Now that the fundamental region of the scene and the shadows has been painted, I work back in the artistic creation beginning with the sky and mists' uttermost zone away. Skies are some of cool tones and the lightest qualities in the scene. I made the sky tones with ultramarine blue, titanium white, and a touch of phthalo green. For the mists illuminated by the sun, I utilized a blend of titanium white and a little consumed sienna.

I painted the region of the mountain in light with similar varieties I utilized in the shadows; notwithstanding, the worth of the variety blend is a lot lighter worth. Titanium white and copied sienna are the prevailing tones in the light dim blend. While painting these zones in the acrylic scene, I remember that acrylic paints dry more obscure, so I consider that by making my variety blends somewhat lighter than they should be.

PAINTING THE GREENS IN THE MID-GROUND

I worked forward in the artwork and blended different greens on my range to convey the vegetation in the scene painting. There is a blend of straw-shaded and green grass on the mountain inclines as well as stands of trees. I blend different greens to make different varieties and tones. While blending greens, it is fundamental to recollect that the immersion of the greens exits the further into the distance you go. Thus, I start by blending a lower chroma green and afterward increment the immersion of the tones as I slowly work up toward the forefront, where the haziest shades of the most soaked greens are found. I blended the different greens utilizing fluctuating mixes of various tones of yellow ochre, cadmium yellow, ultramarine blue and titanium white as my base tone. I added more cadmium yellow and a little phthalo green to build the immersion and I adjusted the greens with either some alizarin red or cadmium red light.

CHAPTER FOUR

PAINTING THE WATER

The water is a fundamental part in the piece as it makes cadence in the work of art and coordinates the watcher's eye toward the mountain. The water mostly mirrors the sky, so I utilized a blend of ultramarine blue, phthalo green, and titanium white. I apply the brush strokes with expansive clearing marks for a more painterly, impressionistic look. Nonetheless, I utilized a few fine subtleties towards the finish of the work of art to add profundity. The edges of the stream bank reflect into the water and I utilized a blend of consumed sienna, yellow ochre, ultramarine blue, and titanium white. I found that the worth of this tone was excessively light, so I obscured it later on as I dove into additional subtleties.

DEMONSTRATING ADDING SUBTLETIES AND REPEATING THE DULL QUALITIES

The quick drying nature of acrylic paints enjoys its benefits, particularly while demonstrating and adding the subtleties in my mountain scene painting. It is extremely simple to begin layering on new paint over existing layers. Basically, I'm utilizing comparable varieties to what I was utilizing when I was obstructing in the painting however am changing a portion of the qualities. For instance, the shadows behind the scenes mountain were excessively dim so I added lighter shades and layers of paint. I added more subtleties to the vegetation in the mid ground, particularly the trees, and afterward I repeated the dim qualities. The little trees in the closer view have some very dull impediment shadows inside them and for this I utilized a blend of ultramarine blue and yellow ochre, making a dim, cool tone. In certain areas, I likewise blended in a little phthalo green and alizarin ruby. I obscure the regions around the banks of the stream with a blend of consumed sienna, yellow ochre, and ultramarine blue. If necessary, the worth can be made lighter by blending in some titanium white.

With the artistic creation dry, I added last subtleties to the mountain and the vegetation. This is likewise an opportunity to add my lightest qualities to this acrylic scene painting. The lightest qualities are in the mists, snow, and the shines in the sparkling water. I added more layers to the mists with a blend of titanium white with a touch of consumed sienna and yellow ochre to make a warm tone. I likewise utilize this tone to add a portion of the features in the snow, which I do sparingly.

I paint the shimmers in the water utilizing titanium white paint with a minuscule measure of yellow ochre. I completed the artwork by adding subtleties to different varieties in the stones in the forefront. The varieties in the stones are changing mixes of various tones of ultramarine blue, consumed sienna, titanium white, and alizarin dark red.

THE END